Codes of a Soul

Yaritza Vasquez

BookLeaf Publishing

Presentation by *BookLeaf Publishing*

Web: www.bookleafpub.com

E-mail: info@bookleafpub.com

ISBN: 9789357440813

First edition 2023

Dedicated to me

ACKNOWLEDGEMENT

Thank you to everyone who has ever inspired love in my life.

Thankful for the gift of Creation and all the beauty that comes with it.

Wonder

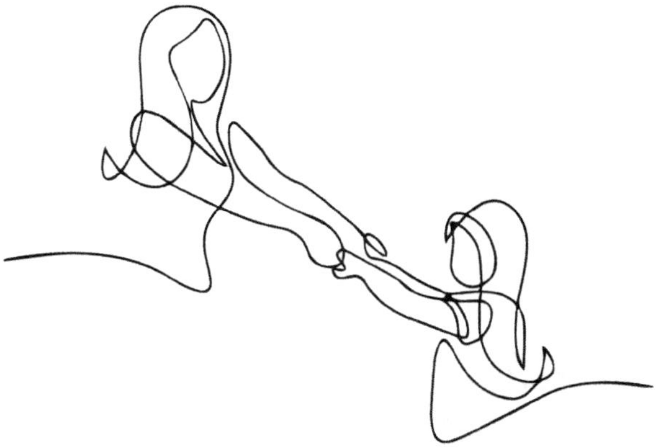

Let me see the world through your eyes
The moon running away from the clouds
The stars like dots on a canvas
Airplanes in the sky like moving buildings
The wonder that gives you focus and makes us
See the things that we've forgotten

Light

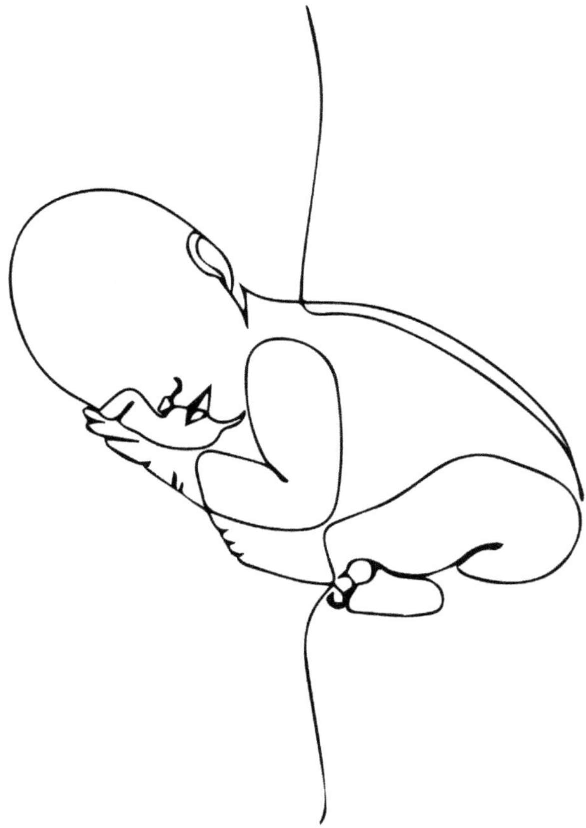

Awaking so close as to feel you exhale
Sweet almonds and vanilla
How could you be this amazing
A wildflower amid the sunshine
The shining light in my window
The worries and hopes of my heart

You've been the greatest experience
There are simply not enough words, languages,
or breaths to suffice
The beauty you radiate into our world
I could write about you for a thousand years
And it would still be too little
to tell of all your light
You divine gift from above
You shake my soul to pieces

Stay you, my dear
For you are always enough
And much more

You are always love
You are always light

Silence

Close your eyes
Hear the silence
The absence of noise makes
The sounds truly count

Love

Words don't exist to explain it
Actions aren't strong enough to show it
Silence doesn't do it justice

The words from deep within that no one else can reach, if not for you and Him

It is everything
that drives us to and from, near and far
A divinely gifted ability
A strength that prevails against weakness
A flaw that yields and carries on

Some say it’s good, others don't
They say we cannot pass it by
Its power can sink so far within
As if to make us nearly crippled
As extreme as to fall into a lifeless dream
They also say it can revive us, heal us
The cause of our existence

An instinct that lets us collapse to our knees but lifts us back to our feet

A sweet heaven to call a home
of sheer bliss and content

If not for it, where would we be?
What would we do?
It drives us, we can feel it close
Causing confusion and ecstasy all at once

A force we could never clarify
We wouldn’t trade it for the world, why?

Because we can clearly see
it’s profound enough to
somehow understand
the deficient words,
the lacking actions,
the unjust silence

A Special Someone

A special someone
What a privilege to know you
To have crossed paths
To live our moments together

A special someone
Whose heart cries the world's tears
Collapsing in thoughts of darkness
Covering the innermost weaknesses
To stay strong

A special someone
Deserving of kindness, unity, belonging

A special someone
Dedicated to love
To give

A special someone
Trying to make sense of it all
To not fully fall

A special someone
What a lovely being
To simply share love
And want to be loved

Lonely Flower

Lonely flower
Why so isolated?

The one to my right has gone away
The wind has blown it toward a path
I cannot follow

Good

You're just so good
There's no other way to explain it
No malice
No ill intent
Pure heart

Kiss me now and never part

Essence of Life

Looking at you two and there just aren't words
You're the essence of life
What an honor to be yours

My eyes light up
And I wonder what I did
To live this reward

Thanks for teaching me
The greatest love
I'll ever know

Loss

How do you get over the feeling of
losing someone?
They were perfect
They were amazing
But now they're gone

It keeps hurting and the pain won't go away
Like salt in a wound
You try talking
You try writing
But you still think about the good ole days

Wishing you could cut out the agony
That would feel so good, wouldn't it?
But there will be scars

Full healing is the ultimate illusion
Instead we will grow
Around the pain, the sadness
We will use it to propel us
Into strength and power

Until our prize arrives

Feel

Sapphire seems to be the color of
everything I see
The sky with its radiant white clouds seems to
travel endlessly
The ocean with its blue glow mysteriously
creeps into my line of sight
I turn my head just slightly as my hair brushes
my shoulder and I look up, now

Jade seems to be the color of everything I see
The trees shine their shadows down on to the
endless fields of grass
Continuing to blow smoothly in the wind
Resembling the strands of my hair
that do the same
The breeze here seems limitless; kissing my skin
as if to say: *"Thank you for being here."*

I smile when it calms
I stare into the horizon happily as if to say:
"You're welcome."

Drowning

The current goes faster
Only to push me along
I feel like I'm
Drowning

No one else can save me
From this misery
Just you

So you finally take me, then
I look away and
You let go

Free

I sit alone in the awkward silence
Dreaming about how I'll fill these blank lines

Not knowing where to start
I then realize
I can feel free to feel free
Now is a new beginning
The choice to express this ability is a gift

The best of what I'm thinking comes together

Sweet Slumber

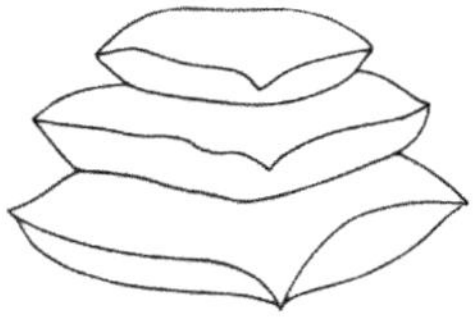

Where are you?
Let me find you because
My mind keeps pulling me away
From the sweet slumber

I need to recuperate
Give me serenity
Let yourself be found

Fly

The mind is a barrel rolling down a hill
It might crash and burn
It might stop
It might go faster

It can feel out of control
When you're not sure what's coming

But if we could tell the future
Wouldn't it defeat the purpose
Of the joys we're meant to experience
Of us proving our strength, our loyalties

Amidst the suffering
There's a lot of good

So help me God
To put away the worry, the uncertainty
Because I could crash and burn

But what if I learn to fly?

Anxiety

At my wit's end
Where do I send my thoughts
I can no longer lend them to another day
I want them to finish, not diminish
Bend the reality of imperfection

But I must come to an acceptance

For now, you're here to stay
You can be too much but you can keep me safe
You give me the strength to find a helping hand

You can be overbearing, but
Can I defeat you?
Absolutely, when I need to.

To Know

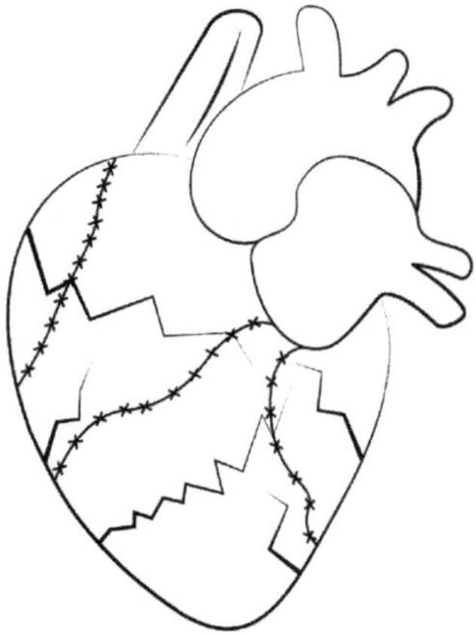

To know love is to know loss
Loss of oneself
Loss of a moment in time

I'm lucky to know love
But the latter is painful

Paint

They say closure is overrated
Maybe it is
Maybe closure is yearning for what we had
Visiting a version of us that passed

I don't think we ever stop feeling for closure
For a feeling doesn't simply disappear
It evolves

The loss of closure is protection sometimes, sure
At what cost?
A life spent wondering what once was, or wasn't
We'll never really know

Trust in the now and be still
Appreciate the beauty the loss of closure
has painted
Be in the moment, stay thankful
Fill your canvas with the moments of a lifetime

Branded

It’s involuntary
The way you resurface

The branded tattoo you’ve left
Marked on her soul
Bleeds tears
Yet embraces her
Tells her to be strong
Be present
For she’s where she’s meant to be

Heal

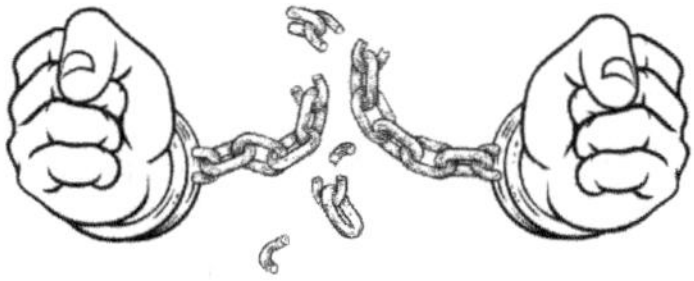

Suppress your feelings
Don't you cry
Bury the trauma

Strong.

Express your feelings
Cry
Grow with your trauma

Weak.

Why is that?
The way I see it
Perceived weakness is strength

Heal.

Lights On

Life is weird

There are days so full of love
And others so full of struggle

Days so full of light
And others full of darkness

It makes you wonder why we're here
It can't have all been for this
Because the gloom tends to overpower

And it's as if electricity is
nonexistent in the world
As if the sun were destroyed to pieces
The mere definition of doom

For love I will keep fighting
To keep the sunshine flowing in
The light switch on

Tainted

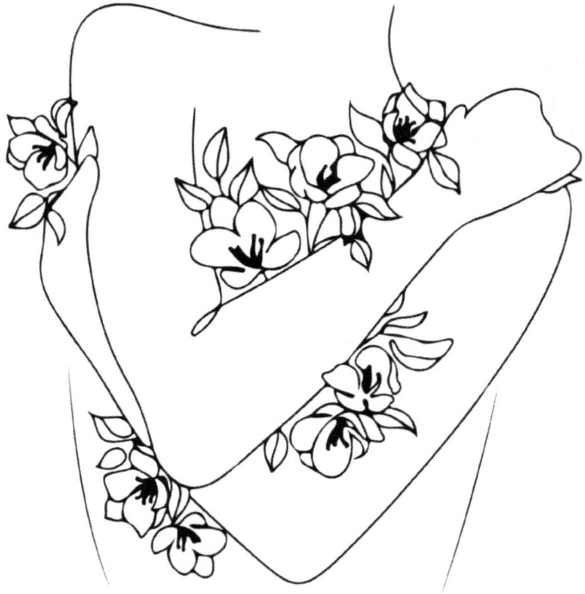

Green, I walk in and it's all I see
It's not what I'm there for
But it's there for me

The prettiest green ever seen
It feels unfair really
A color so vibrant I lose me

My dreams search it on the spectrum
It was greatly flawed
But there was beauty in learning
the novelty of color
Falling for the affection of wide-eyed wonder

Tainted with black, yes
Nevertheless, a prismatic force
Short-lived and long loved

www.ingramcontent.com/pod-product-compliance
Lightning Source LLC
Chambersburg PA
CBHW051751130826
49812CB00033B/1106
* 9 7 8 9 3 5 7 4 4 0 8 1 3 *